They've been
side by side
for sixty years,
so why haven't
The Beano fun-pals
ever met
The Dandy
comic chums?
Wait a sec,
though — read this
tale from a
1989 Beano . . .

TURN TO THE
INSIDE BACK COVER
TO GET TO
THE 'POINT' OF
THIS STORY!

To DREW
FROM BOBBY

**Printed and published in Great Britain by
D. C. Thomson & Co., Ltd., 185 Fleet Street, London.**
© **D. C. THOMSON & CO., LTD., 1999.**

(Certain stories do not appear exactly as originally published.)

ISBN 0-85116-697-0

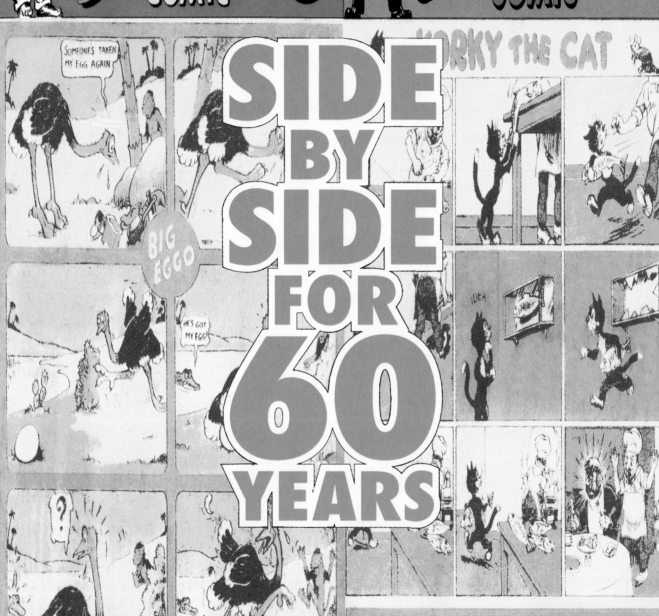

SIDE BY SIDE FOR 60 YEARS

SIDE BY SIDE *in the '30s*

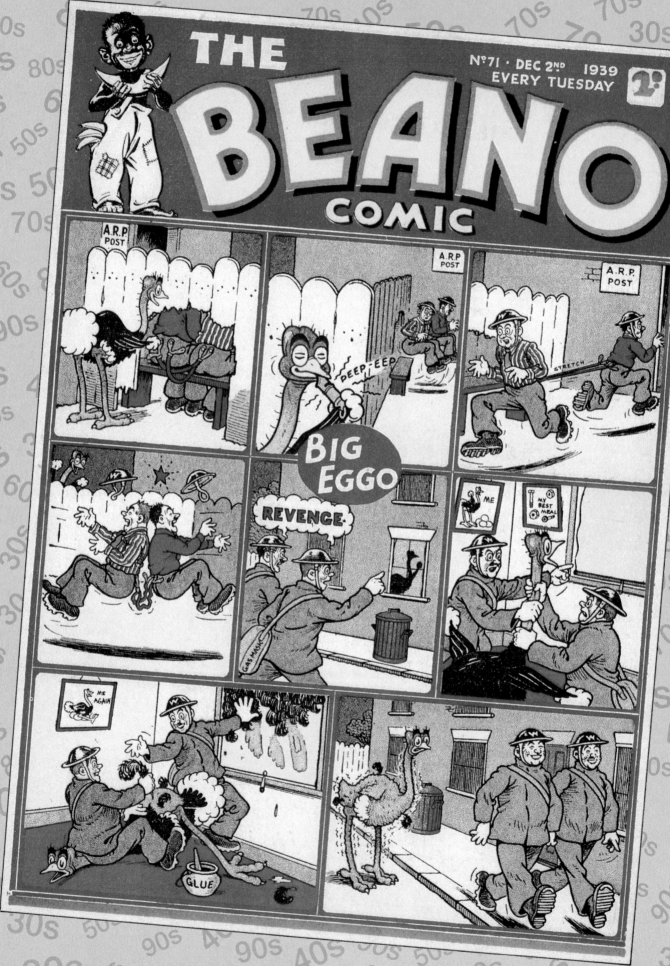

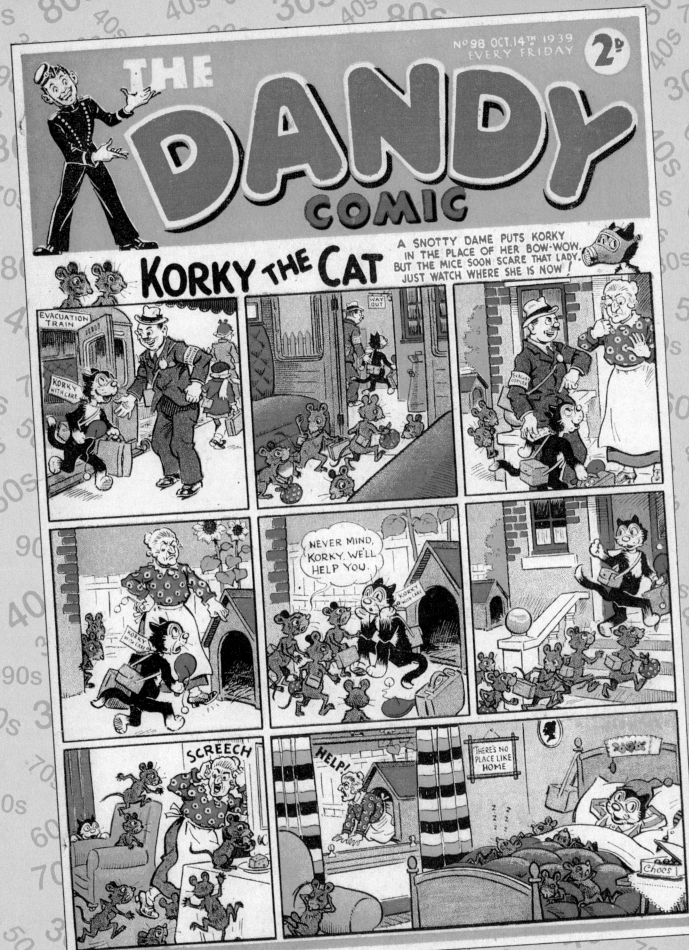

In the early days of Dandy and Beano
Wartime laughs go side by side,
When the mice help evacuee Korky
And wardens dent Big Eggo's pride!

SIDE BY SIDE *in the '40s*

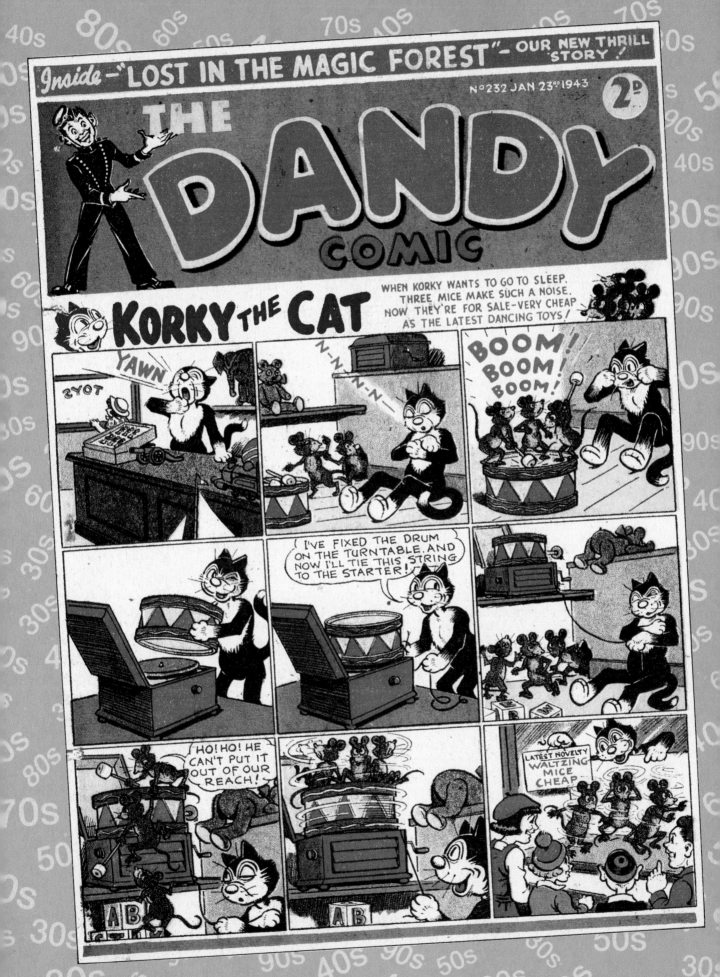

SIDE BY SIDE *in the '50s*

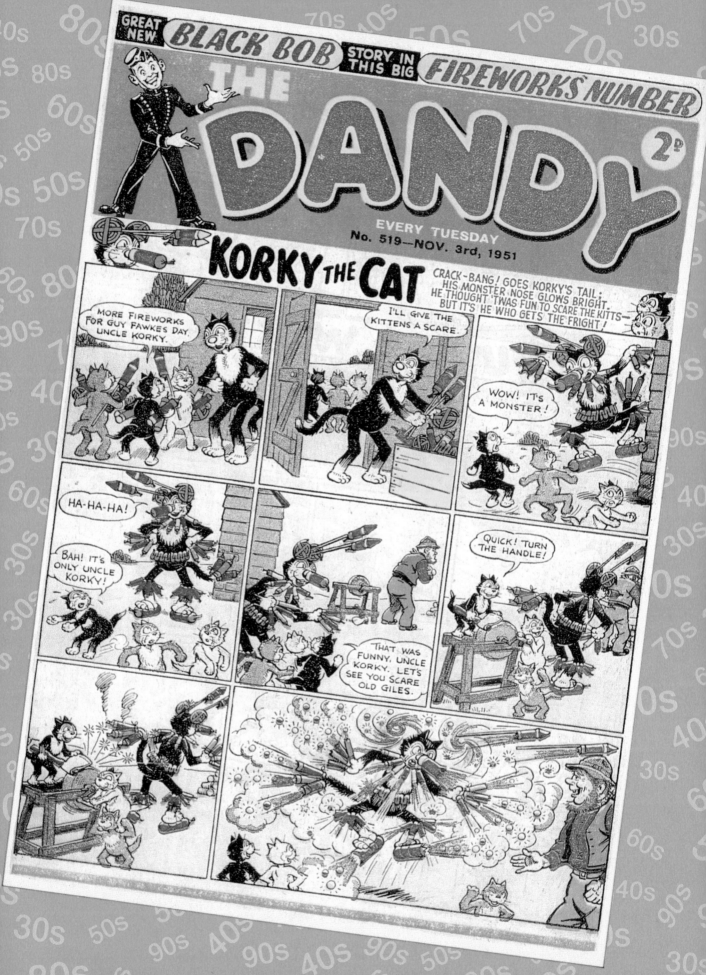

SIDE BY SIDE *in the '60s*

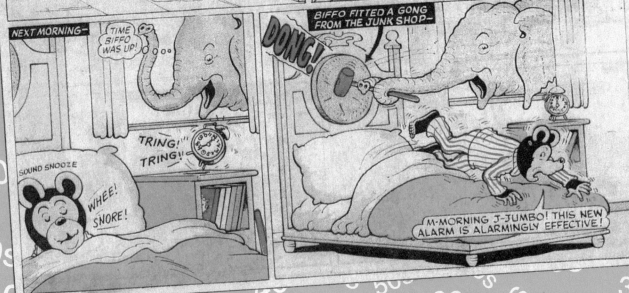

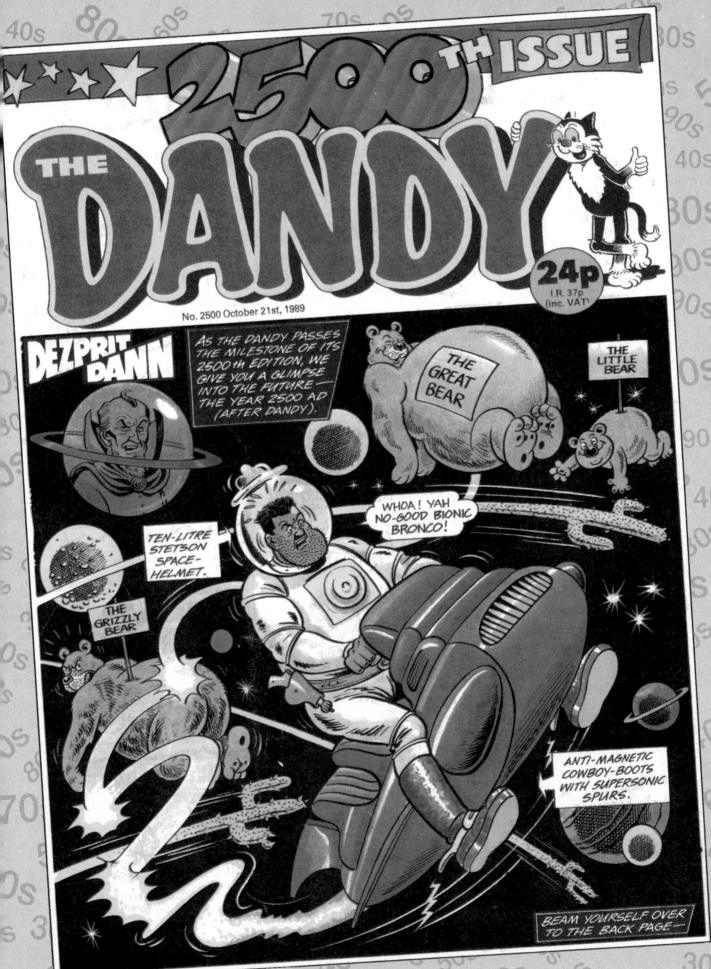

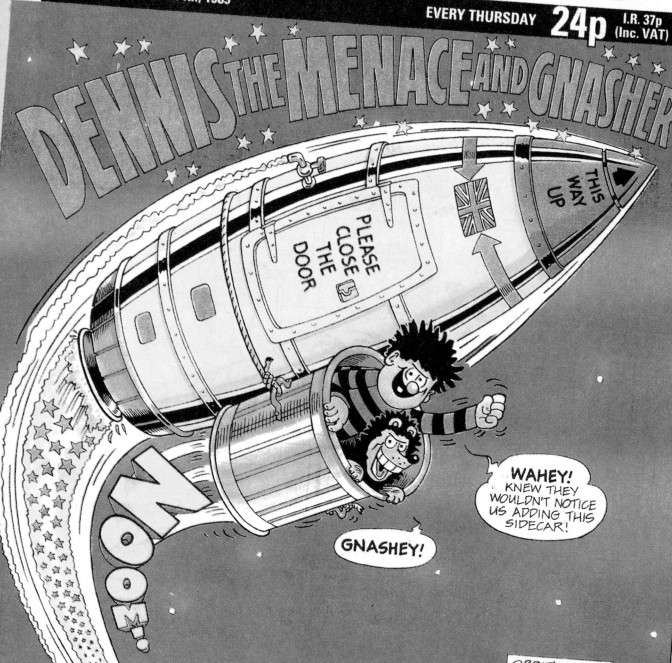

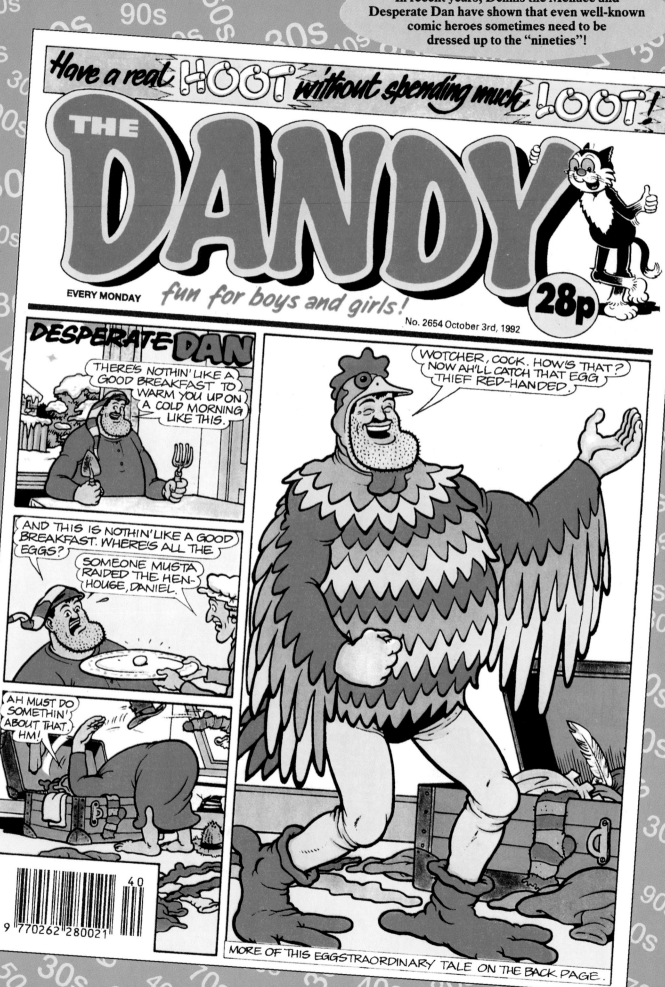

WHAT WAS THE BIG NEWS OF 1998?

Dennis's pal Pieface's birthday? *NO CHANCE!*

The new BEANO CLUB? *NOPE!*

Ivy the Terrible expanding to two pages? *NAW!*

The BEANO web-site? *NO!*

Calamity James baby-sitting a piranha fish? *SIGH! NO!*

WHAT WAS IT, THEN?
Turn over and you'll find out!

HERE'S HOW IT ALL STARTED

Beano readers were even asked to name Dennis' sister through the Internet. Here's the earliest pic of Little Bea!

Winker WATSON

SCHOOLGIRLS! Hundreds of 'em and they were all trooping along outside the walls of Greytowers School, home of the famous, and pleasantly surprised, wangling Winker Watson!

> I SAY, WINKER! HUNDREDS OF SCHOOLGIRLS!

> WHERE ARE THEY GOING?

The girls' teacher looked awfully familiar . . .

> YOU THERE! FETCH MR CREEP!

So, she was the sister of Clarence Creep, Winker's Form Master — and deadly enemy!

> HELLO, BROTHER CLARENCE!

> AGNES, DEAR SISTER! SMOOCH!

Agnes Creep told them that the Girls' School had burned down and they were moving to a new school — Trinity Hall, right next door to Greytowers!

> WATSON! YOU AND THE BOYS WILL CARRY THE GIRLS' BAGS!

So off they all trotted, Winker's brain in overdrive! There had to be lots of wangling opportunities with a Girls' School next door!

> HEY-HO! OFF WE GO! WE'RE THE CREEP FAMILY PORTERS NOW!

Trinity Hall's Matron, Miss Grenfell, was surprised.

> YOU'RE EARLY, GIRLS! THERE'S NO FOOD IN YET!

> WHILE YOU UNPACK, WE'LL RAID THE PANTRY, FOR A SCHOOL-WARMING PARTY!

> GOOD-OH!

> THE PANTRY IS EMPTY!

> I HEAR HEAVY FOOTSTEPS COMING!

Winker was a good boxer — he certainly boxed this intruder!

RUN LIKE FUN!

Agnes Creep was furious — and she blamed her own girls!

FOR BUFFETING ME WITH A BISCUIT BOX, NONE OF YOU WILL GET SUPPER!

WE DIDN'T DO IT!

BISCUITS

CLARENCE, DEAR BROTHER! I'M COMING ROUND. PREPARE A SLAP-UP SUPPER!

While she was on the phone, Winker was raiding Clarence Creep's private pantry!

CATCH, CHAPS!

Winker hid just as the door opened!

BETTER PREPARE SUPPER!

CREEPY!

GOT TO DISTRACT HIM!

CRASH!

TINKLE!

WHAT WAS THAT?

WHO'S OUT THERE?

I'LL CATCH THE LITTLE WRETCH!

OFF YOU GO — NOW I CAN BE OFF!

As the blissfully happy Agnes made her way round to Greytowers, Winker and his pals sneaked into Trinity!

SOME SUPPER, BROTHER! STALE TOAST IN A FREEZING ROOM! BAH!

Meanwhile the welcoming party was in full swing at Trinity Hall, all thanks to the ace wangler, Winker Watson!

TUCK IN, GIRLS! A TWENTY-TWO COURSE SUPPER, COURTESY OF GREYTOWERS BOYS — AND ONE UNWITTING TEACHER!

YOU'RE A BRICK, WINKER!

PEACHES

BEANS

BEANS

Now it's a Minnie the Minx story . . .
Hang on, **THAT'S** not Minnie!

MINNIE THE MINX

LOOK! "BEANO" ONLY 4d!

HMMM!

YOU'RE GOING TO GIVE ME A SWEET, AREN'T YOU?

OH, YOU'LL HAVE TO ASK MY BIG BROTHER, MIN.

WHAT DO YOU WANT, GIRLIE?

ER-ER...

... N-NOTHING! IT D-DOESN'T MATTER! I'M J-JUST GOING!

LATER—

YOU DON'T MIND MY BORROWING YOUR BIKE, DO YOU?

I DON'T—BUT I THINK MY BROTHER MIGHT.

HUH! WHO'S SCARED OF YOUR BROTHER?

THEN—

G-G-GULP!

SO—

BAH! BIG BROTHERS— NOW, IF I WERE BIG AND STRONG...

I AM!

H-E-Y! THAT GIVES CLEVER LITTLE ME AN IDEA.

60

BACK AND SIDES!

Desperate Dan's been troubled by hair restorer too — on his chest!

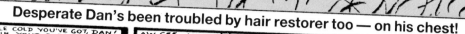

KORKY THE **CAT**

Korky's barber's pole gets bust
On Guy Fawkes Day, in '52
But the acrobats forgot the date
So WHIZZ-BANG !
— and off they flew!

Even before the strip was called "The Bash Street Kids", they were causing adults to tear their hair out! This page is from The Beano in 1954 when the original title was:- WHEN THE BELL RINGS!

DIRTY DICK

COME ON, DICK! YOU'RE GOING TO THE BARBER'S TO GET THAT SCRUFFY MOP CUT WHETHER YOU LIKE IT OR NOT!

AW, DAD!

SO LONG, DICK! DON'T COME HOME UNLESS YOUR HAIR'S CROPPED NICE AND SHORT!

BAH!

GURR! COME HERE, YOU MEDDLING LITTLE BRAT!

HELP!

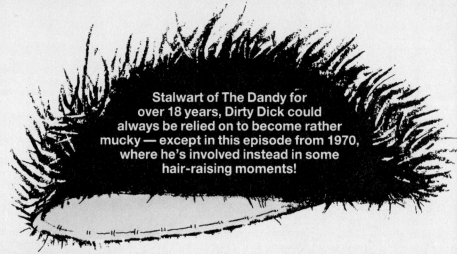

Stalwart of The Dandy for over 18 years, Dirty Dick could always be relied on to become rather mucky — except in this episode from 1970, where he's involved instead in some hair-raising moments!

HERE'S SOMETHING FOR YOU.

A BAG OF TOFFEES! OH, THANKS, DAD!

YUM—YUM! THESE TOFFEES ARE SMASHING!

BLOW

THERE'S A SWEET PAPER STICKING TO YOUR HAIR, DICK. I'LL TAKE IT OFF. WOW! WHAT'S THIS?

OH, CRUMBS!

AT THE BARBER'S

BALDIE & SON

THE BARBER WON'T BITE ME, DICK. COME ON!

D—DON'T GO IN THERE, DAD!

I'D RECOGNISE THAT HAIR ANYWHERE!

HUH! WHAT A LONG WAIT! I'M FED UP. I SAY, WONDER HOW THIS THING WORKS?

BLAST!

OH, GOLLY! I'VE SWITCHED IT ON!

CLICK!

PHEW! I'VE MANAGED TO SHAKE HIM OFF. HELLO! WHAT'S THIS STUCK TO MY SHOE?

IT'S THE BARBER'S WIG, AND IT'S QUITE A GOOD FIT, TOO. WONDER IF I COULD FOOL DAD WITH IT? I'LL TUCK MY LONG HAIR UNDERNEATH.

TUCK

BACK HOME

HOW DO YOU LIKE MY HAIRCUT, DAD?

EXCELLENT, DICK! NICE AND SHORT.

YOU THOUGHT YOU COULD DIDDLE ME WITH THIS WIG, DID YOU? YOU'RE FOR IT, MY LAD!

A WIG! I'VE NEVER THOUGHT OF WEARING A WIG BEFORE.

WONDER IF ANYONE WILL RECOGNISE ME? I'VE A GOOD MIND TO TAKE A WALK AND SEE.

COME ON, DICK—BACK TO THE BARBER'S! AND THIS TIME I'LL MAKE SURE YOU GET YOUR HAIR CUT.

I—I WOULDN'T WEAR THAT WIG IF I WERE YOU, DAD.

NONSENSE, BOY! WHAT DO YOU MEAN?

YOU OUGHT TO BE ASHAMED OF YOURSELF! FANCY GETTING YOUR BOY TO PINCH MY WIG SO THAT YOU COULD WEAR IT, YOU BALD OLD COOT!

60

HO-HO! YOU WERE RIGHT, DAD—THE BARBER DIDN'T BITE YOU, HE JUST MADE SURE THAT YOU WOULDN'T BE BITING ANYTHING FOR A WHILE!!

SIDE-TRACKED!

OFF YOU GO, CORPORAL CLOTT, AND CATCH THE COLONEL AT THE RAILWAY STATION. HE'S LEFT HIS CASE BEHIND!

YOU'VE JUST MISSED THE TRAIN, CORPORAL! YOUR COLONEL'S ON IT!

WELL, HE CAN'T GO ON HOLIDAY WITHOUT HIS CASE!

THROW THINGS AT ME, WOULD YOU? TAKE THAT!

OUCH! A LUMP OF COAL!

HUH! HE MISUNDERSTOOD MY MEANING, THE SILLY MUTT!

COLONEL! COLONEL! HERE'S YOUR CASE!

GET READY TO MAKE A GRAB FOR THE COACH, SIR!

STEADY, CLOTT! DON'T LET ME DOWN NOW!

HELP! I CAN'T GET MY FEET FORWARD. DO SOMETHING, CLOTT!

YES, SIR!

BUT—

HERE! WHAT'S THIS? STEALING A RIDE ON MY TRAIN?

EH? I ASSURE YOU, MY GOOD MAN, THAT...

GOLLY! TROUBLE!

OFF YOU GO—THE WAY YOU CAME ON!

HELP!

THERE'S YOUR CASE, SIR!

SIDESHOW

This unusual three-picture strip shows that even in 1952 Biffo didn't have to speak to raise a laugh — or save some people from a burning building!

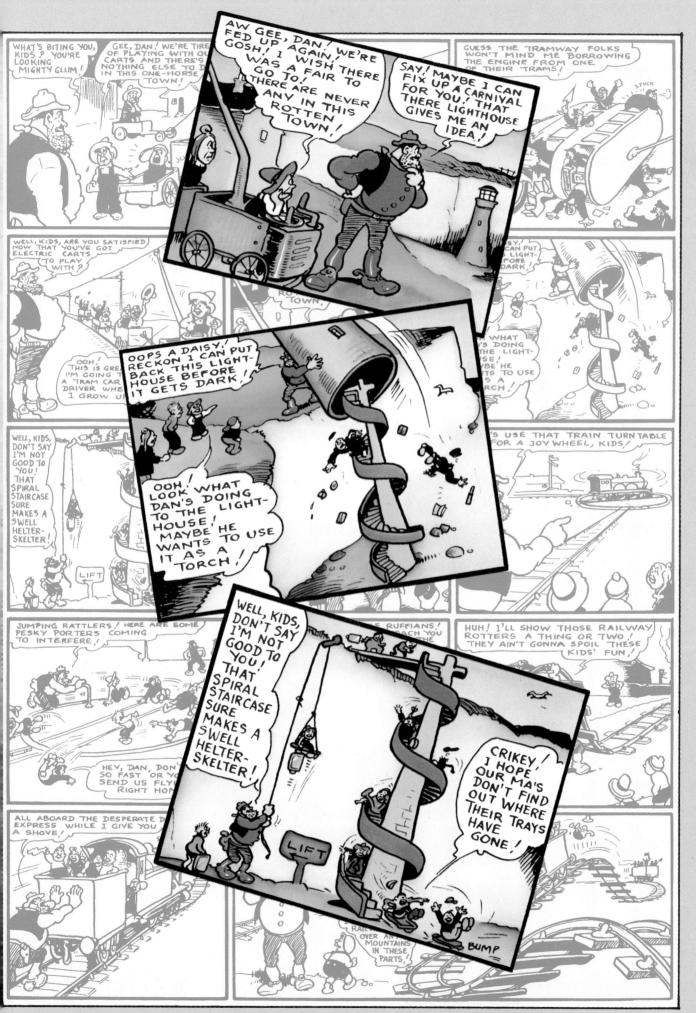

Twelve years previously, Desperate Dan had a very similar idea to Biffo's, but he didn't need a cart — just his own strength. You might say it was a *very* light-house for Dan to pick up!

The Beano is always full of fun for everyone from commoners to kings — as shown by this episode of "Wee Davie and King Willie" from the series which started in the early 1950s.

HELP! THE ROUNDABOUT'S OUT OF CONTROL! THEY'LL BE THROWN OFF!

HELTER SKELTER

LATER THAT WAS JUST WHAT THE DOCTOR ORDERED —NOW WHERE DO WE GO FROM HERE?

TO THE ICE-CREAM FACTORY OVER THE ROAD.

THE ROYAL HOSPITAL

WON'T YOU SAMPLE OUR PRODUCTS, GENTLEMEN?

YOU BET WE WILL!

CRASH

TINKLE TINKLE

TOWN JAIL

THIS IS ONE VISIT I DIDN'T PLAN AT ALL!

A Dandy favourite, **BRASSNECK,** the Amazing Metal Schoolboy, was more of a Metal Mayhem-Maker over three series between 1964 and 1984.

DID YOU SEE THIS, MR SNODGRASS? WE MUST MAKE SURE NONE OF OUR PUPILS GET THEIR NAMES IN THE PAPER!

DON'T WORRY, HEADMASTER! I'M TAKING MY CLASS ON A VISIT TO MALCHESTER STATELY HOME!

DANDY BLAH! SCHOOLBOYS CAUSE TROUBLE AT FUN-FAIR

And that class included Charley Brand and his metal pal, Brassneck . . .

IN WE GO, BOYS! THIS IS MALCHESTER HALL!

I'D RATHER GO TO THE FAIR, CHARLEY!

ME TOO, BRASSNECK!

Shortly—

THIS BEAUTIFUL PORTRAIT WAS PAINTED IN 1723 . . .

FATSO'S A BORE! I'LL SNEAK OFF AND LIVEN THINGS UP!

THIS IS WHAT I NEED!

RUBBISH DUMP

. . . THE HOUSE IS FULL OF VALUABLE THINGS . . .

CRASH!

YIKE! DID I DO THAT?

THAT VASE YOU SMASHED WAS WORTH A FORTUNE, MR SNODGRASS!

I'LL HELP YOU TO HIDE BEFORE ANYONE DISCOVERS WHAT YOU'VE DONE!

And look where Brassneck's taking the tubby teacher!

FUN-FAIR

IN YOU GO, MR SNODGRASS! YOU CAN HIDE IN THERE!

GHOST TRAIN

PAY HERE

NOW, I'LL JUST, ER . . . SPEED THINGS UP A LITTLE!

SLOW
FAST
VERY FAST

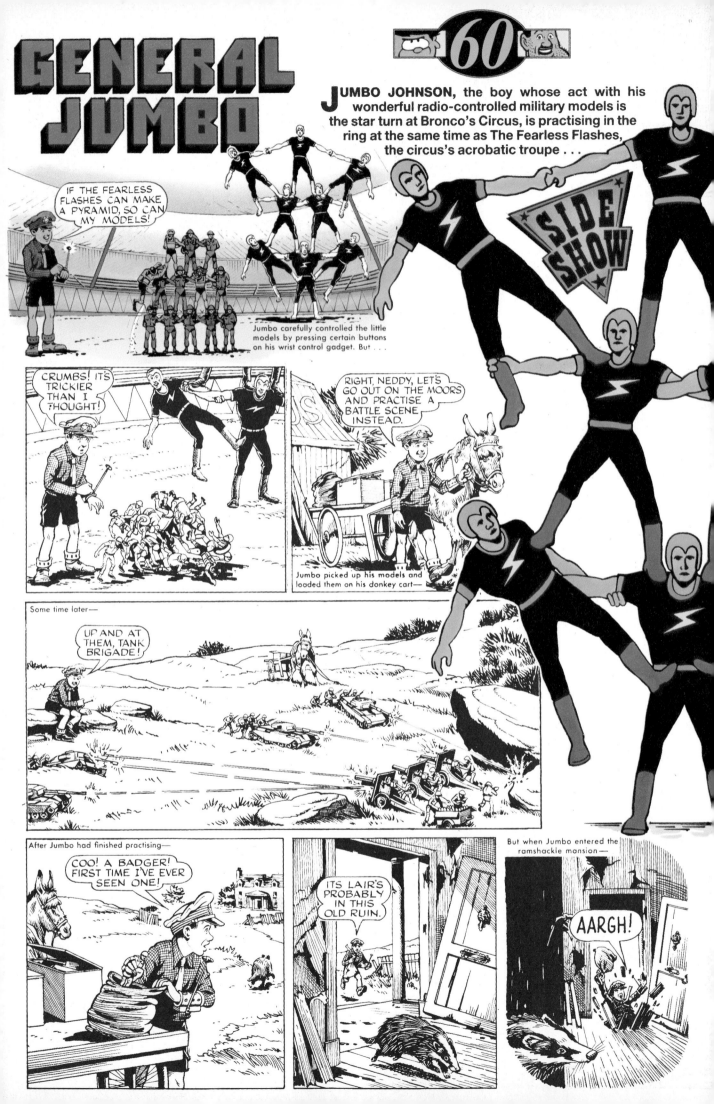

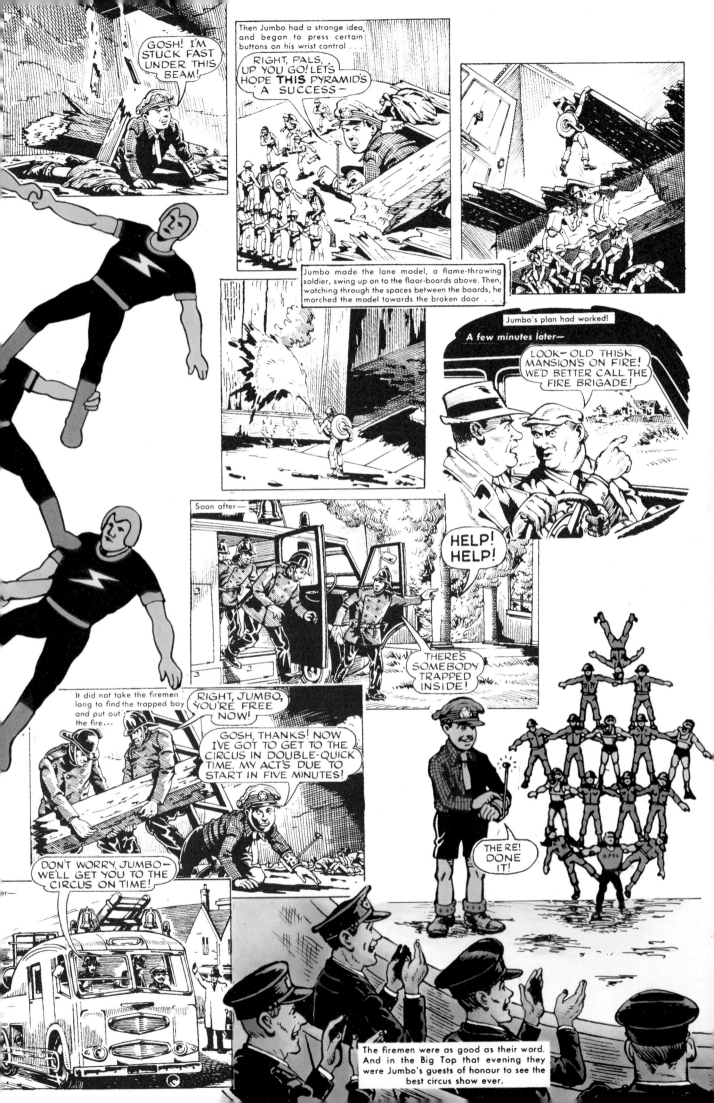

Have you ever tried to stop a giant Crimson Ball with an elephant, in the middle of a fairground? Probably not, but that's exactly what happened in a story from the Dandy Book of 1965!

WHAM! The Crimson Ball rammed into the elephant, hitting it head-on with such force that the great animal was lifted off its feet and hurled bodily backwards for many yards. It crashed into a roundabout, knocking the whole thing off its mounting and scattering the children who had been riding on it. Screams and yells pierced the air. Everywhere panic-stricken people fled.

Follow the fortunes of late '70s *Dandy* character, *Rah-Rah Randall*, and feel free to yell out the **RAHs** and **BOOs** printed in red!

HI, BOYS! I'M A FORTUNE-TELLER, TOO!

GET LOST, CRUNCHER!

MY BALL'S NOT A CRYSTAL ONE...

BONK!

CLOUT!

OO!

OH-OH!

...BUT IT MAKES YOU SEE STARS ALL RIGHT!

BOO!

I SAY! THAT LOOKS LIKE AN EASY WAY TO EARN CASH!

FORTUNES TOLD

HOROSCOPES SUPPLIED 50p.

HURRAH-RAH!

JUNK YARD

LOOK, RANDALL! THAT GOLDFISH BOWL'S JUST LIKE THE FORTUNE TELLER'S CRYSTAL BALL.

AND THERE'S AN OLD CARAVAN. I'VE GOT AN IDEA!

YOUR SCHEME'S MAKING US RICH, RANDALL!

FORTUNES TOLD HOROSCOPES SUPPLIED 10p.

PAY HERE

RAH-RAH!

THE GIRLS HAVE GONE, BUT WE'VE MADE A PACKET!

I'LL WIPE THOSE SMILES OFF THEIR FACES!

KICK!

TIP!

HEY!

NO WONDER THEY CALL IT FORTUNE-TELLING! I'VE GRABBED A FORTUNE!

BOO!

HE'LL BE BACK, BUT WE'LL BE READY NEXT TIME!

LATER—

NO SIGN OF THOSE TWO SAPS! THEY'VE PROBABLY RUN HOME SCARED!

HAW-HAW! I'LL SEE WHAT'S IN THE CRYSTAL BALL.

FORTUNES TOLD HOROSCOPES SUPPLIED 10p.

PAY HERE

EEK! A HAIRY HAND!

TEE-HEE! YOUR MONSTER MITT MADE HIM RUN, BILLY!

HELP!

SIDESHOW

RAH-RAH!

HEY! WHAT'S THIS?

EEK! A HAIRY HAND!

HE WALKED RIGHT INTO OUR TRAP, RANDALL!

YEAH! OUR CRYSTAL BALL WAS A HORRORSCOPE!

RAH-RAH FOR RANDALL!

SIDE BY SIDEBOARD!

IN CLASS IIB —

WHO WOULD LIKE A COUPLE OF HOURS OFF SCHOOL?

US!

SUDDENLY—

BAH! NO WONDER IT WAS SO HEAVY!

WE'LL TAKE A SHORT-CUT DOWN BY THE CANAL, AND ACROSS THE BRIDGE!

THIS WAY TO CANAL

BRIDGE UNDER REPAIR.

BAH! WE CAN'T GET ACROSS THE BRIDGE!

GOAL!

CRASH!

SPLINTER!

GLUE

COULD YOU TAKE THIS OLD THING TO THE DUMP?

TO GRANDAD FROM SMIFFY

D-DUMP? IF YOU'RE THROWING IT OUT, CAN WE HAVE IT?

THE SIDEBOARD HAS ARRIVED, TEACHER-NOT A SCRATCH ON IT!

THANK YOU, CHILDREN NOW STAND WELL BACK!

SCHOOL

60

...O TO PUDNEY'S FURNITURE STORE AND COLLECT A SIDEBOARD FOR ME!

SO—

THAT'S THE ONE.

SOLD

COO! MAYBE IT'S AN ANTIQUE. WE'D BETTER BE CAREFUL.

HM! IT LOOKS HEAVY.

FURNITURE STORE

GROAN! WHAT A WEIGHT! WHERE'S FATTY GOT TO?

THIS'LL GIVE TEACHER'S SIDEBOARD A NICE WASH!

ROVERS F.C.

LET'S STOP AND WATCH THE GAME!

SHOOT!

TEACHER'LL NEVER NOTICE—I HOPE! START PUSHING!

GLUE

BUT—

PUSH! COLLAPSE!

OUTSIDE SMIFFY'S GRANNY'S—

SMIFFY, MY BOY, COULD YOU GET SOME OF YOUR PALS AND DO A LITTLE JOB FOR ME?

OK, GRANDAD!

WRONG AGAIN →

YAHH!

CRASH!

BOILER HOUSE

YES, I THOUGHT THAT OLD RELIC WOULD MAKE GOOD FUEL FOR THE BOILER FIRE!

AFTER ALL OUR BOTHER! GURRRR!

Taking Sides

The Dandy's "Jocks and Geordies" had almost fifteen years of bashing lumps out of each other's gangs before the Dandy editor decided he wanted thump-thing else on their pages!

SIDES

WHAT A FOOTBALL TEAM THEY WOULD MAKE!

Thirty-five years ago, someone on The Beano staff had a bright idea — imagine a football team with twelve copies of Dennis! ARGH! And here's the result! P.S. Dennis's side won!

TAKING SIDES

Twenty years ago, in The Dandy, schoolboy wangler Winker Watson and his chums were up against an unknown enemy.

JOLLY NICE SWEETS THESE! HAVE ONE, TROTTY?

Then Winker realised he was talking to himself. Trotty had disappeared, suddenly and without a sound.

TROTTY? WHERE ARE YOU, TROTTY?

Trotty wasn't far away, but he was a prisoner of the three senior pupils known as the Hoods, who had terrorised Greytowers for months, yet had always managed to keep their identity secret.

WE'VE GOT HIM, WATSON, AND HE'S GOING TO GET HIS ARM TWISTED UNLESS YOU HAND OVER THOSE SWEETS AND ANY CASH YOU'VE GOT IN YOUR POCKET.

OH, NO! I WON'T!

Winker's refusal made the Hoods carry out their threat. Trotty's arm was wrenched up his back.

YELP!

OKAY, YOU WIN, YOU ROTTEN LOT OF BULLIES!

As soon as they got their loot, the Hoods melted away into the woods. But they left Trotty with a very sore arm!

NEVER MIND, TROTTY. MATRON WILL FIX IT UP WHEN WE GET BACK TO SCHOOL.

In sick bay, Trotty had his arm put in a sling while Winker watched.

THANKS, MATRON, THAT'S FINE!

GOSH! THAT GIVES ME AN IDEA...

There was a practice football match that afternoon, and Winker reckoned he could use it to help work his latest wangle.

LISTEN, LADS, HERE'S WHAT WE'LL DO...

During the game, there were lots of accidents—and lots of injuries were caused, especially arm injuries!

OUCH! MY ARM!

CRASH!

OUCH! MY ARM!

The injured players couldn't play on, they must report to Matron at once. And she put a sling on every one of them!

WE'RE READY FOR THE HOODS NOW!

Back in Dorm Three, it became clear what Winker's plan was.

RIGHT! WE'VE GOT OUT OF FOOTBALL, SO LET'S GO AND HAVE A PICNIC.

But as the Third Formers made for the open air, they were suddenly faced by the three Hoods.

TEE-HEE! JUST LOOK AT WATSON AND HIS BUNCH OF WOUNDED SOLDIERS! THEIR PICNIC BASKET IS OURS FOR THE ASKING! JUST PUT IT DOWN THERE AND SCRAM.

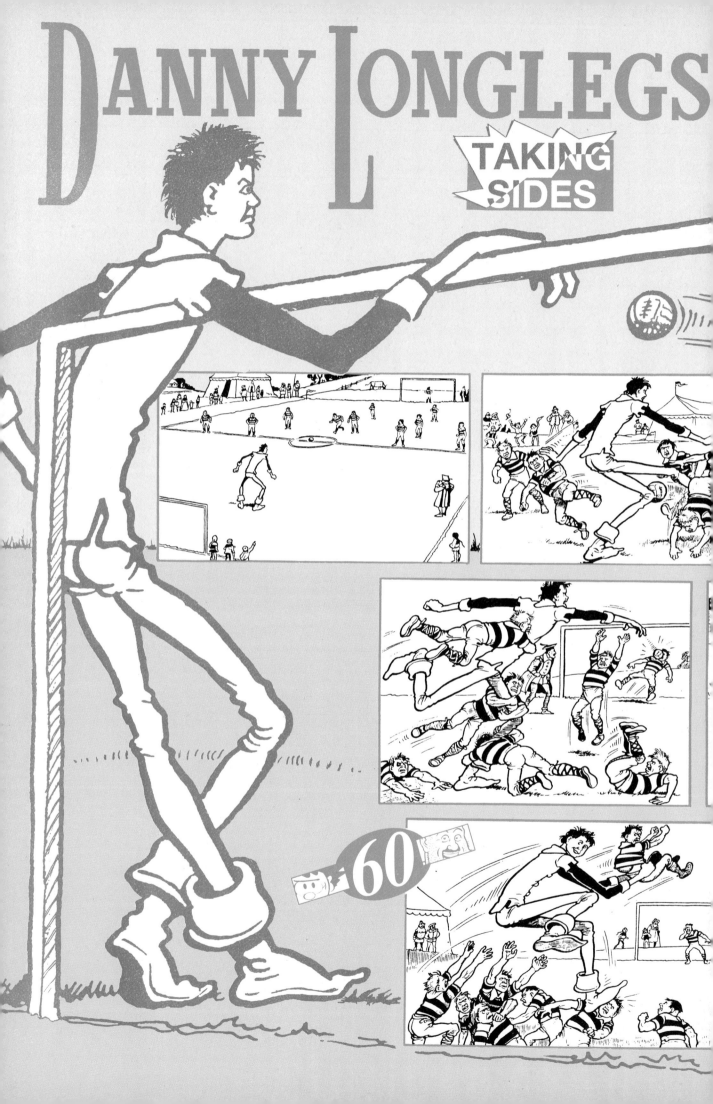

This tale from *The Dandy* of the 1940s had lots of wording under each picture originally, but the twelve pictures tell their own story of how Danny's one-man team took on a full eleven-man side at football!

TAKING SIDES

Hang on readers! Let's think about this! Before you know what they're arguing about please **TAKE SIDES!** Billy or his pal? Done that? Now let's get on with the story: —

OK—HERE GOES!

HOP

HOP

HOP

NO—NOT EVERYTHING!

BUTT

It's not his SIDES Billy's worried about now, I bet!
— Editor.

Ali Ha-Ha, from the Dandy of nearly forty years ago, gave readers a 'broadside' of 'cannoned' laughter with this Baghdad escapade!

ALEZ-OOP!

AND NOW, GENTLEMEN! ZE MOST SPECTACULAR FEAT EVER PRESENTED TO ZE PUBLIC! INTRODUCING—MUSTAPHA TUPH-NUTT—ZE HUMAN CANNON-BALL!

CRUMP

PERFORMANCE OVER, LADS! NOW FOR ZE BANK!

THERE'S ONLY ME LEFT! I GOTTA TRY TO STOP 'EM WITH THIS CANNON!

10 MINUTES LATER OUTSIDE THE BANK—

THEY'RE ALL IN THERE! I'LL LOAD THE CANNON WITH ROTTEN FRUIT AND BAD EGGS FROM THE GARBAGE BINS—THEN BLAST 'EM AS THEY COME OUT!

HORRIBLE PONG

PHEW! WHAT A PONG!

HO-HO! MY LITTLE SCHEME WORKED! I THOUGHT ZEY MIGHT BRING ZE CANNON ALONG—SO I FIXED IT TO BACKFIRE.

ZIS WAY WIZ ZE LOOT, MEN!

BANK OF

AFTER THE MASS ESCAPE—

B-BUT, DAD—!

GR-R-R! I PUT 40 POUNDS OF POWDER IN THIS CANNON! IN 40 SECONDS, YOU'LL BE 40 MILES AWAY, YOU PEST!

BANK

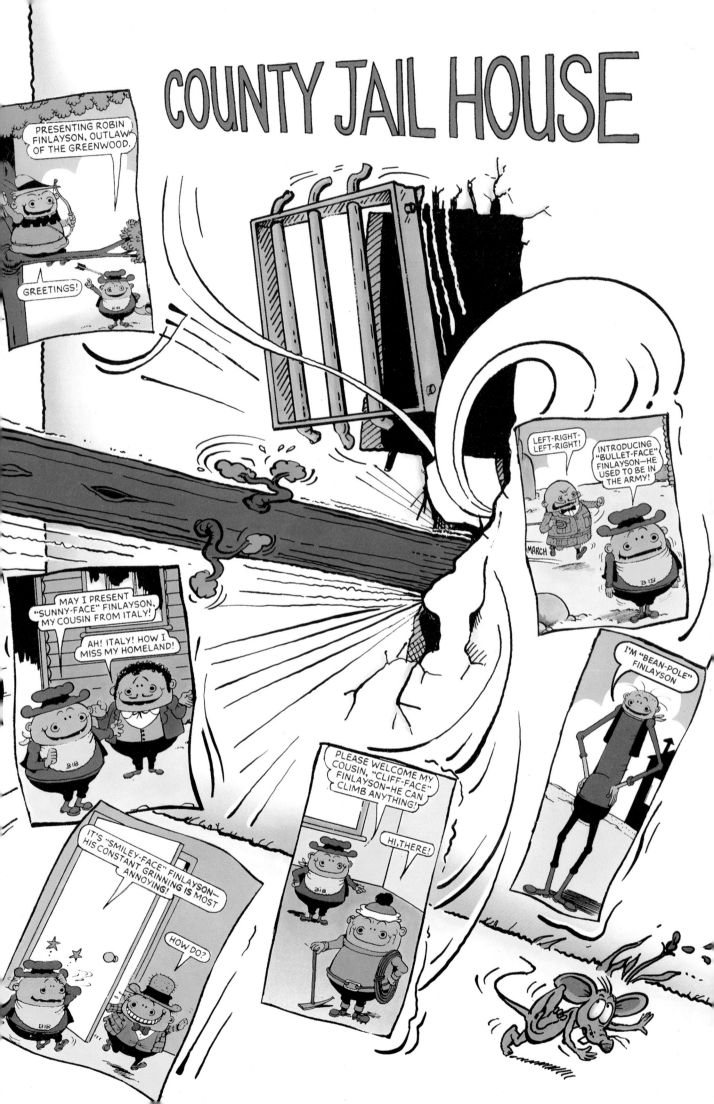

LITTLE PLUM

WISH YOU'D STOP YAWNING, HUBERT—YOU'RE MAKING ME FEEL SLEEPY.
YAWN!

ENTER PLUM'S COUSIN, LITTLE PEACH—
WOULD YOU LIKE UM GO AT FLYING MY 'PLANE, PLUM?
CERTAINLY!

SO—
WHAT UM SPLENDID MODEL!

WHAT A TIRED HEDGEHOG I AM!
YAWN!

HEY!
ZOOM!

CRUNCH!

GRR! YOU AND YOUR PESKY YAWNING!
PHOO!

THEN—
NEVER MIND—LOOK WHAT I'VE GOT!
DROOL! I LOVE CAKES!
SUPER!

YOU CAN SHARE IT WITH ME!
HEH! HEH!

YOWL!
OH! SILLY ME! TITTER!
JAB

GOSH! I DO BELIEVE I FEEL A YAWN COMING ON! CHUCKLE!

GRR! NAUGHTY CREATURE!
SNARL!
DROP
SORE

SHORTLY—
THAT WILL STOP HIS PESKY YAWNING!
MUMBLE!

KORKY the Cat

NIP, LIP and RRIP

Korky's Australian cousin is visiting.

NOT A BAD SCOFF, KORKY, OLD SPORT!

I'VE GOT A SPECIAL TREAT FOR YOU!

UPSIDE-DOWN CAKE!

YUMMO! AN AUSSIE FAVOURITE!

Korky's cousin has his own boxing kangaroo!

HAVE A SLICE, SPORT!

YUMMO!

And the kangaroo has boxed Korky's cheeky nephews

LET'S TEACH THE KITS TO THROW A BOOMERANG!

HERE YOU ARE, SPORTS!

?

IS THIS WISE?

IT'S EASY!

HURL!

WHOOSH!

ZIP!

But when the kits try —

THUD!

TINKLE

CRACK!

CRASH!

NOW UNCLE KORKY'S THROWING THINGS!

RAGE!

HOP!

Korky's throwing a tantrum —

GRR!

GRR! HAVE YOU SEEN THOSE KITS?

KITS! I AIN'T SEEN NO KITS!

THE LITTLE PERISHERS!

CHUCKLE! SNIGGER!

Ever wondered who Biffo's forebears were? Now's your chance fo find out! These masterpieces are from 1969.

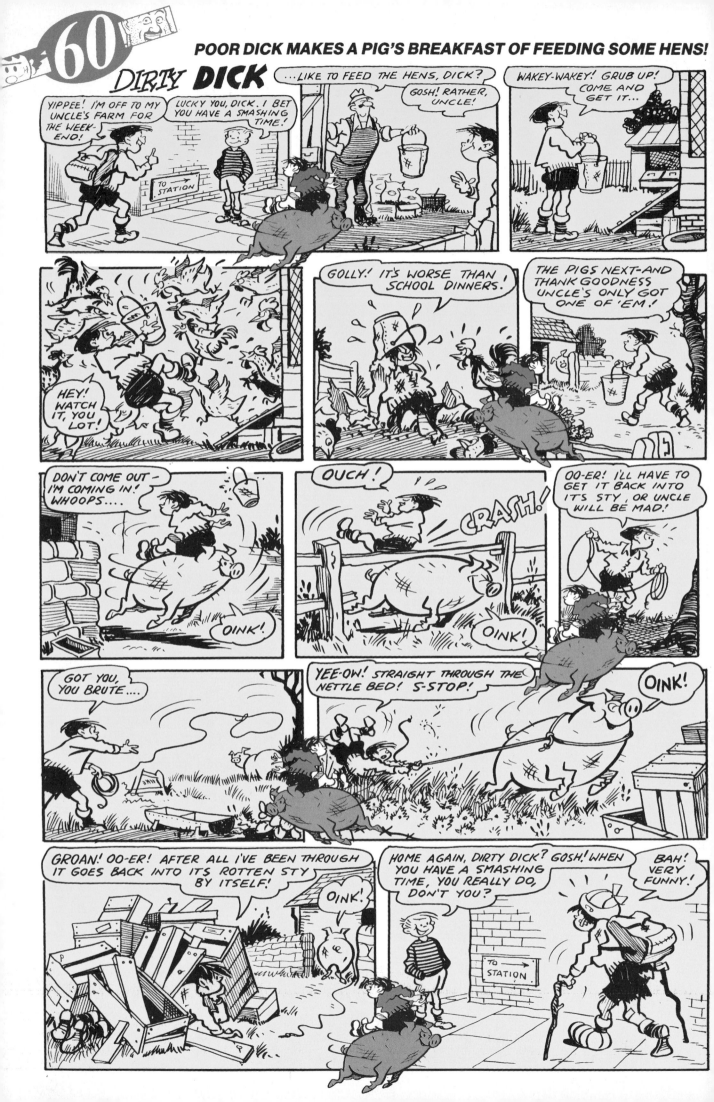

HM! DAD GAVE ME A JOB AND I CAN'T REMEMBER WHAT IT WAS.

HUH! IT'S TIME MY POCKET MONEY WAS RAISED—I'LL HAVE TO DROP A FEW GENTLE HINTS TO DAD.

SO—

GASP! PANT!

WHAT'S WRONG, ROGER?

I'M WEAK WITH HUNGER! PERHAPS IT'S BECAUSE I DON'T GET ENOUGH SWEETS...

WEAK FROM HUNGER INDEED! AFTER ALL YOU ATE AT LUNCH-TIME! GET OUT!

SHORTLY—

YAK! YAK!...RISING PRICES...YAK! YAK!

IDEA!

MINUTES LATER—

PRICES GOING UP!

OH! THAT REMINDS ME, ROGER...

YES, DAD?

I MUST GIVE MUM MORE HOUSEKEEPING MONEY!

BAH!

LATER—

HM! THERE ARE TOMMY AND BENNY WITH THEIR NEW BIKES.

DAD! COME AND SEE THIS!

WHEN MY DAD SEES MY PALS WITH NEW BIKES—HE'LL FEEL MEAN AND GIVE ME MORE POCKET MONEY.

WHAT'S THAT?

GET AWAY, YOU LITTLE HORRORS!

ULP! WHAT'S THE MATTER WITH DAD?

ROGER!

ULP!

Y-YES DAD?

YELP!

I TOLD YOU TO MEND THAT FENCE SO THOSE DOGS COULDN'T GET IN AND RUIN MY GARDEN! I WAS GOING TO RAISE YOUR POCKET MONEY, BUT AFTER THIS...

MY POOR PUSSYKINS IS STUCK UP THAT TREE! BOOO!

NOW THEN, AUNT FANNY, DON'T FRET. WE'LL RESCUE YOUR CAT. SCREWY! GET A LADDER.

RIGHT, DAD.

STEADY, LAD. YOU'RE NOT AS YOUNG AS YOU USED TO BE.

CRA-ACK!

YEOWL!

OOH! HELP!

HULLO! DAD'S DISAPPEARED. WONDER WHERE HE'S GONE?

I'M HERE, YOU FOOL! I FELL INSIDE THE TREE~ IT'S HOLLOW.

I CAN'T REACH HIM!

GRANDAD HAS CLIMBED UP TO RESCUE DAD.

HERE! I'VE GOT THE END OF THE WELL-ROPE. I'LL LOWER YOU INSIDE THE TREE. GRAB HOLD OF DAD, AND I'LL PULL YOU BOTH OUT.

HOLD STILL WHILE I TIE THE ROPE AROUND YOUR ANKLES.

I'LL LOWER GRANDAD INSIDE THE TREE NOW.

PHEW! THIS IS HARD WORK, PULLING THEM OUT!

A-A-A CHOO!

GRANDAD'S SNEEZE LETS DAD DOWN BADLY!

SPLAT!

HOLD THE LADDER STEADY, DAD, WHILE I CLIMB UP TO UNTIE GRANDAD'S ANKLES.

HUH! HE DESERVES TO BE DROPPED LIKE I WAS.

SNAP!

OH! HELP! THE BRANCH HAS BROKEN!

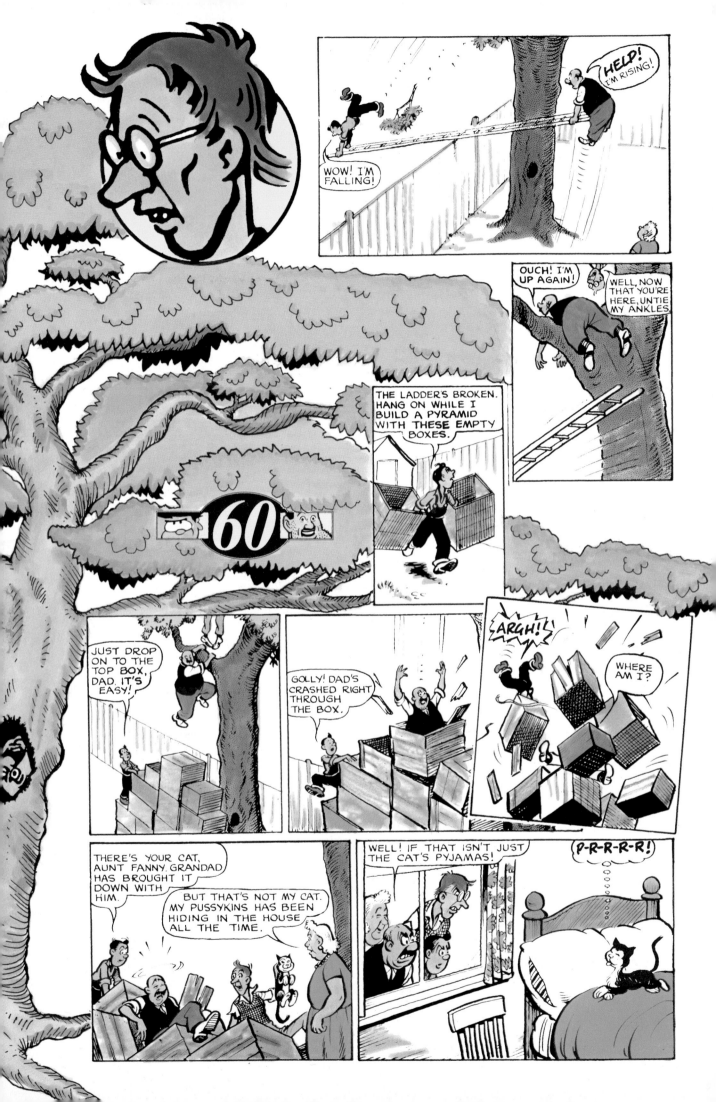

Oh, oh! Who's this? Find out the STAGgering truth farther down this **Lord Snooty** page.

ANGUS, YOUR PET STAG, HAS BEEN DISTURBING THE PEACE IN THE VILLAGE, MY LORD! KEEP HIM UNDER CONTROL!

WE WILL, CONSTABLE!

FROM NOW ON, YOU'LL STAY IN THE CASTLE, ANGUS!

SHORTLY—

HAVE YOU TAKEN OUR TRAMPOLINE, BOYS? IT'S DISAPPEARED.

TRAMPOLINE? OH, NO!

I THOUGHT SO— ANGUS IS TRYING TO GET OVER THE WALL!

BOTHER!

PEOING!

YOU WON'T ESCAPE!

JAIL

PROD

THERE! THAT LEAD SHOULD KEEP HIM OUT OF MISCHIEF!

BUT—

HELP!

EEK!

OH, NO! WHAT'S HAPPENED?

UNTANGLE US AT ONCE, STAG!

CASTLE GUARD

COOK

SNORT! I'LL HAVE TO BE REALLY TOUGH WITH YOU, ANGUS!

LATER—

COME ON!

?

GULP! THEY'RE GOING TO SEND ME AWAY FROM BUNKERTON! SOB!

BUNKERTON STATION

PLATFORM 2

HEH! HEH! WE SENT FOR ANGUS'S DAD TO KEEP HIM UNDER CONTROL!

D-DAD!

CRINGE

34100

LOOK AT OUR NICE, WELL-BEHAVED PET NOW, READERS!

HA-HA!

Hi, 3 Bears fans — that's Uncle Bert in the circle . . . or is it Pa Bear? Let's get down to bear facts in this 1970's Beano story —

EEK! I'M SEEING DOUBLE!

DON'T PANIC, CUB—IT'S ONLY UNCLE BERT!

DOES UNCLE BERT EAT AS MUCH AS YOU, PA?

NO—I EAT NOTHING BUT ANTS' EGGS, TED.

FETCH UNCLE BERT A GOODIE, TED.

YOU'LL SURELY MANAGE A TOFFEE, UNCLE BERT?

I CERTAINLY WILL— I'M YOUR PA!

SOON—

I'LL SIT BESIDE UNCLE BERT AT TEA. PA USUALLY SNAFFLES MY GRUB, TOO!

BUT—

YOU WON'T PINCH MY GRUB, WILL YOU, UNCLE BERT?

I WILL, YOU KNOW— I'M YOUR PA!

IDEA

LATER—

SLURP! I SMELL FRIED ONIONS!

ANY MINUTE NOW!

SNAP!

HOWL!

HO! HO! I CAN TELL THEM APART NOW, READERS. PA'S GOT A BIG RED NOSE!

TWITCH

60

SIDE by SIDE by SIDE by SIDE by SIDE by SIDE!

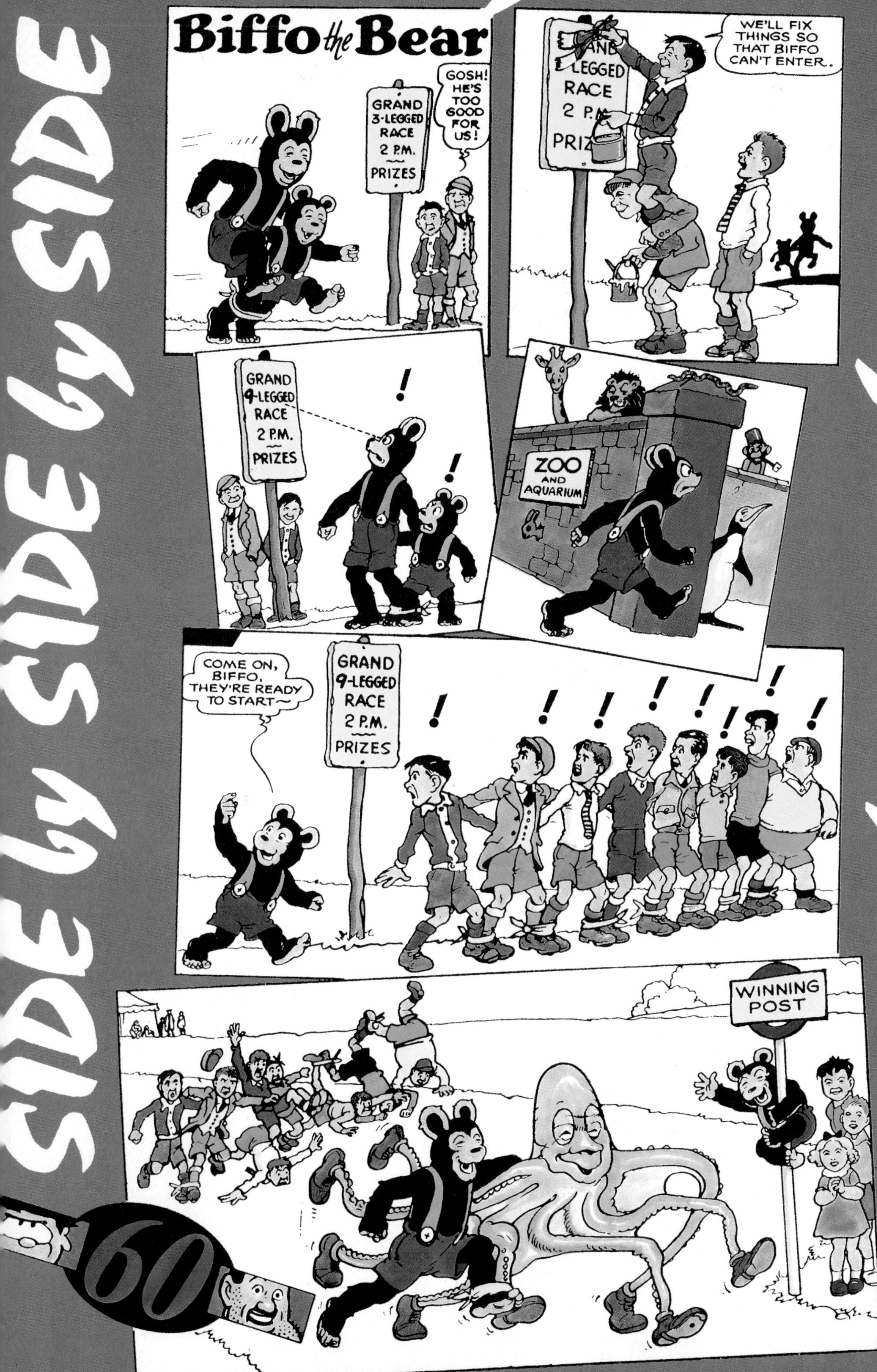

ACHHHHH! IT'S 'IM!

WARNING ALL SHIPS! JONAH IS ON THE LOOSE AGAIN.

Jonah, the Beano's ship-sinking sea-goon of the late '50s and early '60s, is one of an elite few characters who have "jumped ship" and joined the crew of another comic. He began doing what he was best at (sinking ships!) in The Beano back in March 1958, staying aboard for over four years. Then, lost at sea for quite some time, he scrambled on to the deck of the 'good ship Dandy' in 1993. Here he is, starring in two ship-shape tales, which appeared in The Beano and The Dandy over thirty years apart!

THE SUBMARINE "KIPPER" GLIDES SILENTLY BENEATH THE WAVES.

COR! WHAT A PERISHIN' LIFE —

— COOPED UP DOWN HERE IN THIS SARDINE TIN AN' NEVER SEEIN' THE LIGHT O' DAY! I MUST HAVE BEEN CRACKERS TO JOIN UP WITH THIS CRUMMY LOT!

THINK YOURSELF LUCKY, A.B. MOANER —

ABLE SEAMAN JONAH, LIVING WITH THE FISHES JUST BECAUSE I SUNK A FEW DOZEN SHIPS. PHOOIE!

OW!

WE DON'T WANT YOU EITHER, MATE.

That's enough about cats — it's the dogs' turn now! You'd think that the Menace's favourite mutt, Gnasher from The Beano, and Black Bob the Wonder Dog from The Dandy, would never have met — but you'd be wrong! They appeared side by side in a Beano Library (Number 33) back in 1983, as this section shows:-

BEDSIDE MINNIE

In this story from 1967, the ever-pesky Minnie the Minx tries to get on the "bedder" side of Dad!

MY BED'S NOT COMFY, DAD—MAY I HAVE A NEW ONE?

ALL RIGHT. HOW ABOUT A HAMMOCK?

GOODNIGHT, READERS!

ERK!

SUPER!

NO, I DON'T REALLY FANCY A HAMMOCK, DAD.

WELL, WHAT ABOUT A BRASS BED-STEAD? THEY'RE THE HEIGHT OF FASHION JUST NOW.

HO-HUM! TIME TO GET UP.

NOW WHERE ARE MY SLIPPERS?

WAH! WHERE'S THE FLOOR?

OOF!

NO, I DON'T FANCY THAT EITHER—BUT I WOULDN'T MIND ONE OF THOSE BEDS THAT FOLD INTO THE WALL.

WOW!

GOODNIGHT, PALS!

BUT—

MUFFLED HOWLS!

ON SECOND THOUGHTS, I LIKE MY OLD BED AFTER ALL, DAD!

COME ON, READERS — LET ME IN ON THE SECRET AS WELL! WHAT ON EARTH MADE HER CHANGE HER MIND?

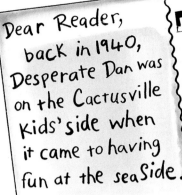

Dear Reader, back in 1940, Desperate Dan was on the Cactusville kids' side when it came to having fun at the seaside.

OUR READERS
ENNY TOWN
ENNYWHERE

BOO-HOO! WE CAN'T GET TO THE SEASIDE THIS YEAR, DAN!

THAT'S TOUGH KIDS, BUT DON'T WORRY, DESPERATE DAN WILL FIX THINGS FOR YOU!

HUH - THESE GUYS LOOK AS IF THEY WANT TO SHARPEN THEIR KNIVES ON ME. RECKON I'LL HAVE TO GET OUT OF THIS BEFORE STARTING TO WORK!

I'LL JUST TUNNEL BENEATH THE SPHINX!

HA! HA! HIM HEAP AFRAID, BURROW LIKE RABBIT!

HALFWAY ACROSS THE ATLANTIC AGAIN!

THERE'S A U.BOAT! ONE LAST BLOW OUGHT TO FIX MY SANDSTORM! I GOT OTHER BUSINESS TO ATTEND TO!

DON'T SUPPOSE HITLER WILL MIND IF I BORROW ONE OF HIS U.BOATS

OER WOW! DER HELP! WE ARE IN DER GRIP OF DER TERRIBLE SEA MONSTER! HEIL HITLER!

NOW I'LL FIX THESE TWO OLD ANCHORS ON TO THE TAIL!

SANDSTORM

GEE! JUST GOT HOME IN TIME! THERE'S THE SANDSTORM BEGINNING TO LAND.

TO CACTUSVILLE 1 MILE

GEE! THIS IS SWELL! AND REAL SALT WATER! TOO!

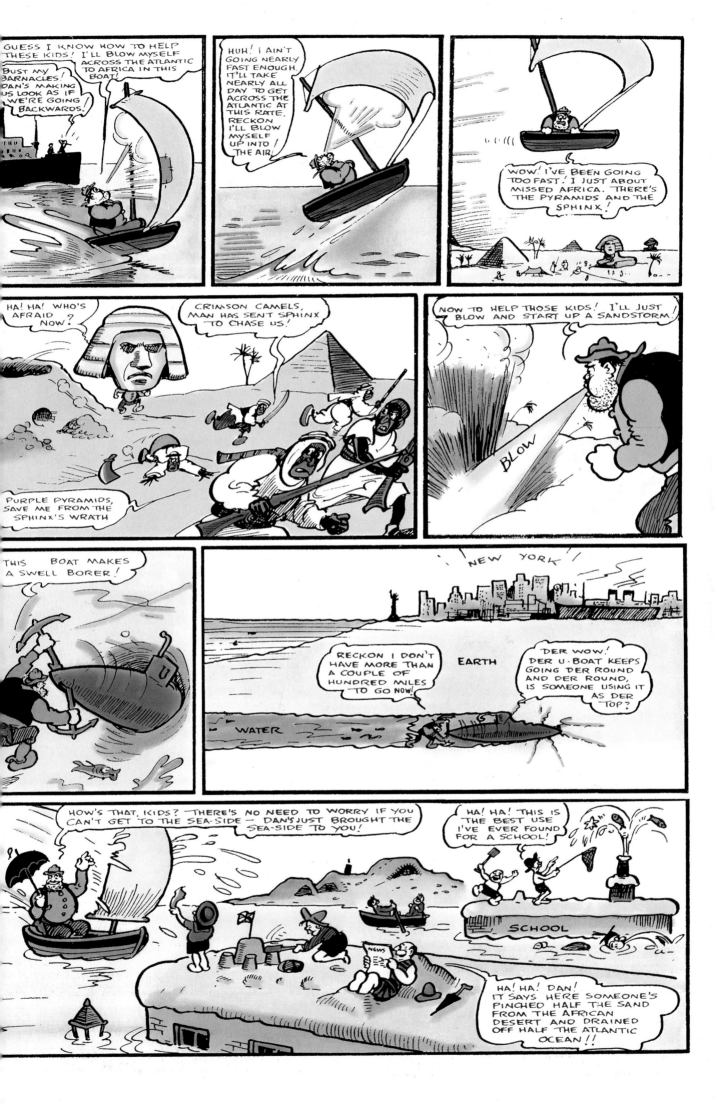

We never see Teacher's face, but every week he was face-to-face with this class-full of horrors in "WHACKO!" a Dandy tale from the '80s . . . but was that the 1780s or the 1980s?!

SEASIDE MENACE

Sun, sea, sand, spade, rubber horse — and a Menace!

Here are two pages of coastal chaos with this 'beach bounder' from the early '60s!

WHAT'RE YOU DOIN' DOWN THERE, DAD? YOU SHOULD BE BUILDING SANDCASTLES LIKE ME!

I'M NOT GOING TO SPANK YOU AND UPSET THE OTHER PEOPLE ON THE BEACH. PLAY AT SOMETHING ELSE!

I COULDN'T HAVE DROPPED IN AT A BETTER TIME!

OOH! HE'S LANDED IN OUR ICE-CREAM!

THANKS FOR THE LIFT, FATTY!

YOUR HORSE'S DAYS ARE DONE, MY BOY!

YOU'VE DRIVEN EVERYONE OFF THE BEACH — SO NOW I WON'T UPSET ANYONE IF I SPANK YOU!

HO, HO! IT'S AMAZIN' HOW A LITTLE SAND IN MY PANTS DEADENS THE PAIN!

CENSORED FOR 60 YEARS

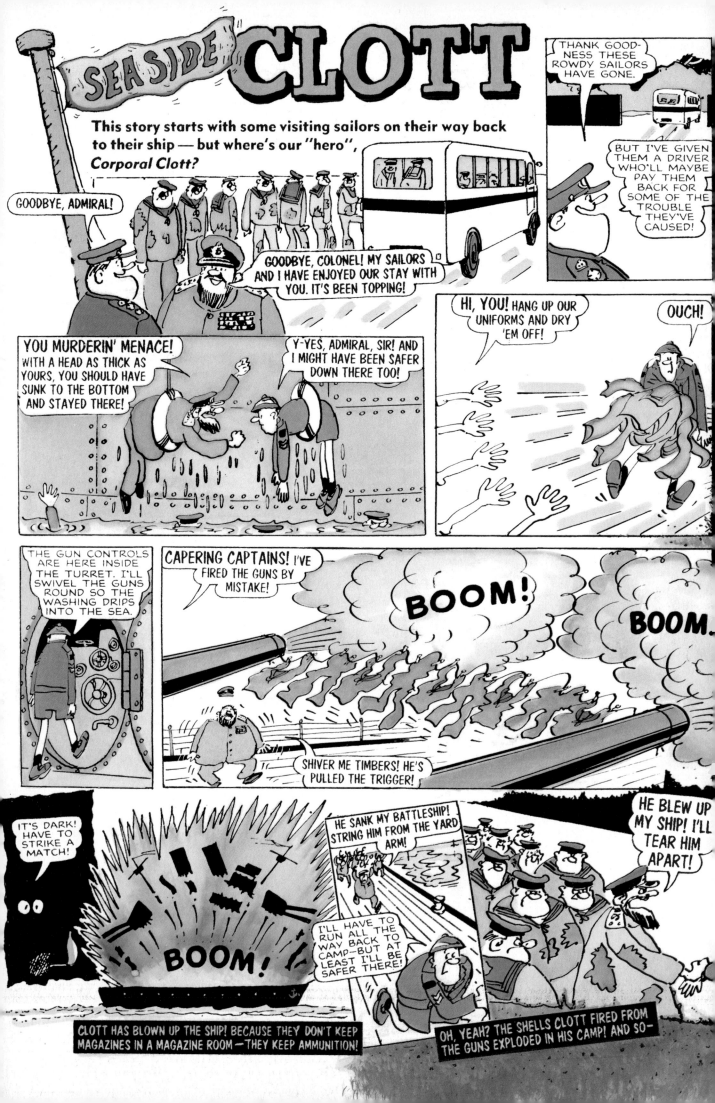

Some characters in The Beano and The Dandy have been in the comic spotlight for only a brief period, before readers' polls gave them the "thumbs down". Here are some who have been

SIDELINED!

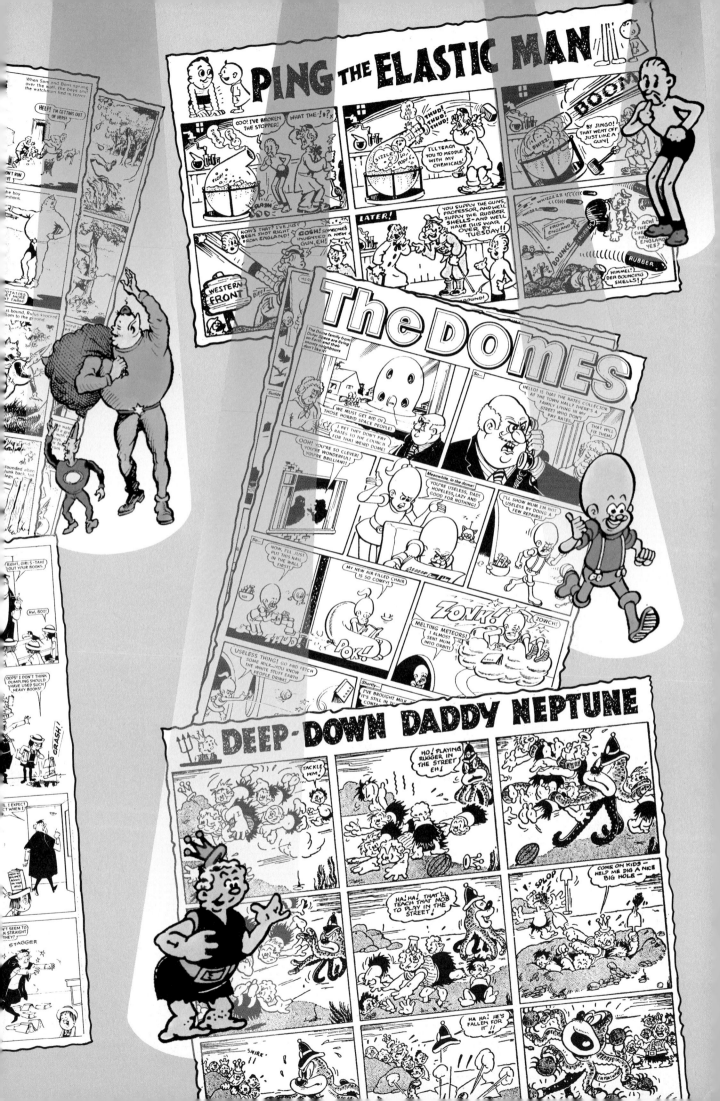

BULLY BEEF and CHIPS

BIFFO AND BUSTER

Throughout most of his reign on The Beano cover, Biffo the Bear had a human pal, called Buster. Although he made hundreds of appearances, poor Buster's name never appeared alongside Biffo's on the title — *until now!*

SIDEKICKS

Unlikely sidekicks they may be, but Jimmy Watson and Strang The Terrible (both from '40s Beano) starred together in an episode of Jimmy's Magic Patch from The Beano dated June 3, 1944.

1 — Jimmy Watson was in another fine pickle! His Magic Patch had landed him in a country where prehistoric monsters roamed. As he looked around him, a huge brontosaurus reared its ugly head above the trees. With great speed for its size it started towards our horrified pal, and he rushed madly in the opposite direction towards a deep chasm. Panting, red in the face, he reached it at last and madly rushed across.

2 — Even then the roars made by the huge beast sent cold shivers down his spine. Luckily it couldn't cross the narrow bridge and slunk off. Jimmy pulled out his handkerchief and sat down on a large stone. Mopping his face, he looked at his comic again. "Gee!" he said. "This might be okay for a bloke like Strang, but it's too much for me." Suddenly Jimmy stopped thinking. The stone he was sitting on had moved.

3 — His heart pounding madly like a sledgehammer, Jimmy felt himself lifted into the air. He had been sitting on a huge triceratops. It was a good job for Jimmy the brute didn't know he was there. As the huge beast, with two large horns sticking from its head, rose to its feet, Jimmy didn't know what to do. Thrusting his comic into his pocket, he thought about jumping off, but suddenly the huge animal started to run.

4 — At that moment Jimmy noticed another monster racing full speed toward the animal he was kneeling on. Now the triceratops was going like an express train towards its opponent. It looked as if Jimmy might be squashed to pulp when the monsters met. Just as he was passing underneath a tree and the two monsters were yards from each other he put his hand over his eyes and waited for the sickening impact.

5 — A second before the beasts clashed together, Jimmy felt himself being lifted into the tree. As he looked above him he saw he was held by the long hairy arm of a gorilla. "Out of the frying pan into the fire!" Jimmy thought as he saw its ugly face peer down at him. The two huge animals were now fighting some distance away and the gorilla hauled Jimmy up on to the branch on which it sat.

6 — The unlucky lad shuddered as it showed its huge yellow teeth. He probably would have been better off where he had been a few minutes before, he thought. Just as he was wondering what was going to happen to him next, the gorilla stood on a branch and, dangling Jimmy in space by his leg, beat on its massive chest with its other clenched fist. To Jimmy it seemed as if the gorilla was challenging someone to fight.

7 — That was just what happened! On the other side of a small stream Strang the Terrible stood. He had heard the challenge from the ape and now he noticed Jimmy dangling from the gorilla's hand. Clenching his fist, he beat on his broad chest, too, returning the challenge. Jimmy brightened up a little as he heard the world-famous strong man. It looked as if he still had a chance. Quickly Strang went into action.

8 — He started to run towards Jimmy and the ape taking huge strides which seemed to be yards long to Jimmy. Jumping the stream as if it were a mere trickle of water, Strang plunged into the thick undergrowth and in a remarkably short time reached the tree. Snarling with rage the gorilla climbed from the tree, dropping Jimmy on one of the lower branches. He gave a startled cry as the gorilla swung out at Strang.

9 — Jimmy needn't have worried. Strang cleverly dodged the swing and closed to grapple with the gorilla. Jimmy watched in horrified silence as the fight went on. Slowly but surely it seemed to Jimmy that Strang was gaining the upper hand, until at last no doubt was left in his mind. Jimmy saw Strang's muscles tense, then, swinging his arm back with lightning speed, he gave the gorilla an uppercut.

10 — The thud of the blow could have been heard for a long distance. The gorilla's head snapped back with the tremendous punch. Its neck was broken, and the lifeless body measured its length on the rocky ground, where the huge bulk lay motionless. Strang was victorious! He helped Jimmy on to his shoulder, and, tossing his school cap in the air, Jimmy cheered until he was hoarse. "Stop that awful row!" grinned Strang.

11 — "Tell me how you got here in the first place." Jimmy started to tell about the Magic Patch but he never got far. Suddenly he realised he was speaking to himself. He was back at home in modern times again, sitting back at the table with his comic in his hand just as he had been reading it before. "Oh, well," he said to himself, "I suppose I'll just have to be content reading about Strang again."

In The Beano of the 60's, Chiefy, of the Smellyfoot Tribe, had reservations about his old totem pole. So his sidekick, Little Plum, got the job of finding a new one. Then Little Plum got HIS sidekicks to help . . .

WHAT DO YOU THINK OF MY NEW TOTEM POLE, CHIEFY? IT'S UM SMASHER, EH? I'LL BE OVER TOMORROW TO PAY YOU UM VISIT.

NEW

PRIDE

HE JUST WANTS TO COME OVER TO BRAG ABOUT HIS NEW TOTEM POLE, AND SNEER AT OUR OLD ONE. I WANT YOU TO GET ME UM NEW TOTEM POLE BY TOMORROW, PLUM!

LATER—

ALL YOU NEED NOW IS UM COAT OF PAINT, PALS, AND YOU'LL LOOK LIKE UM GENUINE TOTEM POLE. CHIEFY MIGHT GIVE US—

BUT—

TICKLE

SLIGHT BREEZE

TEE-HEE!

—UM BIG REWARD!

HELP!

CHORTLE!

WE'RE OFF, PLUM! YOU'LL HAVE TO GET UM TOTEM POLE SOME OTHER WAY.

IN CACTUSVILLE—

AH! UM VERY THING!

NOVELTY BALLOONS

WHAT ABOUT UM NEW TOTEM POLE, PLUM?

I'VE GOT DOZENS OF THEM HERE!

GATHER ROUND, BRAVES! PLUM'S JUST HAD UM MARVELLOUS IDEA! I WANT EACH OF YOU TO TAKE UM BALLOON AND BLOW IT UP!

WOW! UM WHOLE VILLAGE IS FULL OF UM TOTEM POLES!

UM BRAVES ARE UM PUFFED OUT!

ENVY

GASP!

60

FLIP-SIDE FLIP-SIDE FLIP-SIDE FLIP-SIDE

The pages in this section are all living proof that comic pages can sometimes be rather *STRANGE!* Take, for example, this *Jocks and Geordies* story from *The Dandy 1989*. Normally the two schoolboy sides meet in an ordinary, quiet, everyday, modern town, but this particular week . . .

Hear ye! Hear ye! Yea, verily, tis a tale of a Celtic goblin fighter, a fearsome dragon with tonsils of fire . . . or is it an overgrown sea-slug?

A long time ago—

I AM THE FAMED CELTIC-GOBLIN FIGHTER, CEDRIC DE GEORDIE — EL CED FOR SHORT!

AND HERE ARE SOME GOBBLIN' CELTS BY THE SOUND OF IT!

PASS ME SOME MORE PORRIDGE, ANGUS!

SECOND HELPIN'S O' HAGGIS, ECK?

ANOTHER BOWL O' COCK-A-LEEKIE, ANYBODY?

YEEOOW!

JAB!

SCRAM, LADS. IT'S EL CED. HE'S BARBECUED MA SPORRAN!

ERK!

RUN!

WE'LL BE SAFE IN OOR HUT!

YE JOCK HUT

But—

WHIT HUT? EL CED'S FLATTENED IT!

HI HO, SILVER. OOPS! WRONG CENTURY!

OOH! THAT'S A TERRIBLE KNIGHT-MARE!

McMerlin's Cave

WE NEED McMERLIN THE MAGICIAN'S HELP!

This page is "totem"ly ridiculous — you'll have to turn it on its side to read the last picture!

INSIDE CHIEFY'S WIGWAM—

BRR! IT'S CHILLY TODAY.

BUT—

COUGH! SPLUTTER!

GRR! UM SMOKE CAN'T GET OUT OF UM WIGWAM!

OH, OH! I'M OFF!

PLUM!

I KNEW IT!

MAKE UM CHIMNEY FOR UM WIGWAM.

WHY IS IT ALWAYS ME?

SO—

PUFF! ONE OF THESE DAYS I'M GOING TO EMIGRATE FROM THIS PAGE!

LATHER

SWEAT

LATER—

GREAT! LET'S SEE HOW IT LOOKS FROM UM OUTSIDE.

EEK! YOU'VE SPOILED UM LOOK OF UM WHOLE VILLAGE!

GET IT DOWN!

W-WAIT! UM CEMENT HASN'T SET!

SWIPE

SO—

WHEE-E-E-E!

CRASH!

IT'S UM GOOD THING UM ALUMINIUM TOTEM POLE IS SO TOUGH!

OHO! I'VE GOT UM IDEA!

I USED UM HOLLOW TOTEM POLE TO MAKE UM CHIMNEY THAT'S SURE TO BLEND WITH UM SCENERY!

TURN UM PAGE SIDEWAYS NOW

60

FLIP SIDE

"What's going on ear?"
you might say in this
rather strange Biffo
story from 1977.

FLIP-SIDE FLIP-SIDE

One of the oddest stories in The Dandy of the '70s and '80s was this sideways glance in the direction of science fiction, called JACK SILVER, who was a youngster on the planet of Marsuvia. Marsuvia is the wacky world far off in outer space where almost anything can happen. Curly Perkins, a schoolboy from Earth, was a guest here, of his pal Jack. One day, an unusual notice caught Curly's eye —

WHAT DOES THAT NOTICE MEAN, JACK?

THAT? OH, YOU'LL PROBABLY FIND OUT IN A FEW MINUTES!

MOUSERS WANTED
GOOD RATES OF PAY
APPLY

HOI!

GERROUTOFIT, YOU SQUEAKY LITTLE HORROR!

The baker explained his problem to the chums.

MY SHOP IS OVERRUN BY MICE. I'VE TRIED EVERYTHING, BUT I CAN'T GET RID OF 'EM.

MAYBE I CAN HELP.

Jack took Curly along to see an elderly relation of his whose house was full of strange musical instruments.

THAT'S RIGHT, UNCLE ZILAZ. IT'S THE TOOTLEHORN I WANT TO BORROW.

LOOK AFTER IT WELL, YOUNG NEPHEW!

Back at the baker's shop, Jack began to play a weird tune on the tootlehorn.

The music had an instant effect on the mice. They stopped their nibbling, and began to follow Jack Silver.

WHAT AN AMAZING INSTRUMENT!

HA-HA! HE'S JUST LIKE THE PIED PIPER OF HAMELIN!

HELP! MICE!

THAT'S GREAT, JACK! YOUR UNCLE COULD MAKE A FORTUNE WITH THAT TOOTLEHORN.

More and more mice flocked from other shops to join the procession following Jack. He waded into the river, and the mice plunged in after him and were swept away.

But someone was watching as Jack and Curly got their reward from the baker.

I COULD USE THAT THING!

This was Captain Zapp, Marsuvia's most notorious outlaw, and he was plotting.

AND I KNOW HOW I CAN LAY HANDS ON IT!

Captain Zapp leaped on to a Space Scooter.

Two seconds later, Jack and Curly got a terrific shock when the yellow man swooped noiselessly on them from out of the blue.

I'LL TAKE THAT TOOTLER, YOU MUGS!

HOI! GASP! IT'S CAPTAIN ZAPP!

The evil traitor zoomed across the city towards the zoo.

NOW, LET'S SEE . . . I THINK I KNOW THE RIGHT NOTES TO PLAY.

Willie Willikins reckoned he was the luckiest kid in the world! He didn't have an ordinary dog or cat as a pet — he had a Pobble, a Bong Bird (plus chicks) and a WUM! What on earth are they, you may ask . . . and for the answer (sort of!) here's the very last episode of "Willie Willikin's Pobble" from The Dandy of 1952!

WILLIE WILLIKINS was out for a walk with all his pets. He rode on the back of his favourite one, the Pobble, while the Bong bird's four chicks wandered here, there and everywhere. These funny creatures lived with Willie, and where they came from no-one knew, for they had all landed from a mysterious space-ship. Now, as they heard a thrumming noise overheard, they all looked up. But the Pobble soon looked down again, for from the sky dropped something that conked him on the head! Willie gasped. It was a monster lollipop!

2 — He did lots more gasping in the next few minutes, for a torrent of sweets now fell from the clouds — sticks of rock, sweetie pies, toffees, chocolate, long rolls of candy and outsize jelly beans! It was a wonderful surprise for Willie and his pets. When the Pobble recovered from his blow on the napper, he ran and picked up a bunch of the goodies. So did the Bong bird and the WUM. Willie looked up. Sure enough, there was an aircraft overhead, the kind of space-ship which had brought all these odd pets to Earth in the first place. It was dropping the sweets.

3 — Dogs and cats came haring up, following the trail of sweets as they dropped from the speeding space-ship. Willie saw that it was coming lower, and he guessed it was about to land on the waste ground near Reilly's dairy farm. "Maybe it's bringing another pet for me," Willie said excitedly. "Come on, Pobble, let's run." But the others were already running, loading themselves as they went with lollipops and candy bars. A great clatter came from behind as a cart-horse took up the chase.

4 — The sweets from the sky seemed to attract everything on four legs. The cart-horse was only one of many animals that came tearing along to snatch a share. The Bong bird nipped aboard the cart to get to the space-ship more quickly, but she was flung off when the horse slid to a sudden stop. It seized a huge lollipop with its big teeth, and as the WUM had already grabbed that lollipop, a great tug-of-war began. Meanwhile, the Bong bird fought with a dog over a stick of rock.

5 — But the WUM didn't bother much about the lollipop. It gave up the struggle and went chasing on behind Willie. A few minutes later, the long creature got a nasty shock, when a plank suddenly fell on his back. "Umm-m!" it cried, turning to see what had done this. Now it got another shock, for it was Rajah, the circus elephant, which had broken away from the menagerie tent and battered down the fence to get at the sweets!

6 — Willie's pets didn't like being treated rough. As soon as the elephant's weight was off that plank, the WUM wriggled free, and then it coiled itself up like a spring — and sprang! It dived straight at Rajah and hit him in the midriff with its head, with such power that the four-ton monster was toppled on its side. It crashed like a felled tree, and the WUM snatched the stick of rock it had been carrying in its trunk, and made off.

7 — By this time the space-ship had landed on the open ground, and a great crowd gathered round it, men, women, boys and girls, even a policeman. The copper tried hard to keep order. "Stand back!" he roared, but he might as well have tried to stop the tide coming in! Dozens of boys had seen the goodies dropping from this strange flying-machine, and they wanted some. One of them got the sliding door open, and a whole mob of them squeezed inside. But Willie's Pobble wasn't standing for that. He set about laying down the law in his own way — by jerking the boys out of the space-ship by the scruff of the neck! What a hullaballoo there was. The runaway horse, now carrying the whole Bong family as passengers, pulled boys out so that it could get in. Then Rajah arrived and, pushing with all his four tons, almost flattened a crowd of men.

8 — Willie's Pobble worked really hard yanking boys out of the ship, but a fresh half-dozen tried to sneak in again for every one he pulled out. "Pobble-pobble-pobble!" he growled, and the Bong birds and the WUM tried to answer his call. They pushed and wriggled through the crowd till they could get into the machine, and the policeman used his long arms to make a barrier to keep a bunch of sweet-hungry people in check.

9 — At last, some of Willie's pets got through the crush. They fought their way into the space-ship and beat off invaders with lollipops and sticks of rock. Every boy was turfed out, but just as the Pobble was about to hop aboard, a stout guy in a check suit tried to climb in, too. "Pobble-pobble!" grunted the Pobble, and his big paw pushed the man's face. He fell backwards — but then another intruder rushed. It was Rajah!

10 — That was a big task for the Pobble, trying to stop Rajah's rush, and to push the great elephant back. "Bong!" cried the Bong bird from inside, to encourage him. The WUM rumbled "Umm-m!" And that was the last Willie heard of these two strange pets of his, for the sliding door of the space-ship suddenly slammed shut, and to Willie's horror, the engine roared into life and the space-ship took off, into the sky!

11 — "Where have they gone?" Willie said in surprise. Then it dawned on him that all these sweets must have been dropped to lure his funny animals towards the space-ship, and into it. The whole thing had been a trap to kidnap them and take them back to where they came from. "Gee, I'm lucky the Pobble didn't go, too," said Willie to himself. The WUM and the Bong birds were gone, but he still had the only Pobble in the world!

CONTINUED FROM INSIDE FRONT COVER.